THE BABYLONIANS

THE BABYLONIANS

ELAINE LANDAU

THE CRADLE OF CIVILIZATION
THE MILLBROOK PRESS
BROOKFIELD, CONNECTICUT

Cover photograph courtesy of Vanni/Art Resource, N.Y.

Photographs courtesy of Tor Eigeland: pp. 2-3; The Oriental Institute of the University of Chicago: p. 16; The Granger Collection, New York: pp. 18, 45; Giraudon/Art Resource, NY: p. 25; North Wind Picture Archives: pp. 33, 38, 48-49; © British Museum: pp. 34-35, 42; Scala/Art Resource, NY: p. 34 (bottom); The Pierpont Morgan Library/Art Resource, NY: p. 40; SEF/Art Resource, NY: p. 50.

Library of Congress Cataloging-in-Publication Data
Landau, Elaine.
The Babylonians / Elaine Landau.
p.   cm.   (Cradle of civilization)
Includes bibliographical references and index.
Summary: Examines the history of the Babylonian empire and the evolution of its society, including the progressive legal code of Hammurabi, the development of valuable trade routes, and contributions in art, science, and other areas.
ISBN 0-7613-0216-6 (lib. bdg.)
1. Babylonia–Juvenile literature. [1. Babylonia.] I. Title.
II. Series: Landau, Elaine. Cradle of civilization.
DS73.2.L3   1997
935–dc21   96-46871   CIP   AC

Published by The Millbrook Press, Inc.
2 Old New Milford Road
Brookfield, Connecticut 06804
http://www.neca.com/mall/millbrook

CONTENTS

For Michael, who's the best …
better than the rest …

THE BABYLONIANS

IN THE BEGINNING

Thousands of years ago there were no cities, countries, or governments as we know them today. Instead, small bands of people roamed the Earth living off the land. They were hunters and gatherers who were always on the move in search of wild game and fish as well as fruits and nuts to eat. These individuals didn't think of themselves as having a home-land. They were nomadic, or wandering, groups guided in their travels by the need to find food to survive.

No one knows precisely how or why things changed. What made some people trade the freedom to follow the animal herds for the strenuous task of tilling the soil? Although there are no definite answers, a number of theories have been suggested.

Historians note that at first just a few people may have separated from the wandering band. These were probably the weaker or smaller individuals who might have found it difficult to keep up with the rest. In addition, those who had been scorned or were unhappy with the group for some reason may have started to drop out as well.

It is also thought that women possibly played an important role in families settling down. Giving birth to and caring for young children while on the go must have been extremely difficult. Once women realized that remaining in one place would be best for both their offspring (children) and families, they may have been a powerful force behind this change of lifestyle.

There are numerous other unanswered questions as well. For example, when did the process of growing one's own food or planting and harvesting crops begin? Did a specific incident or change in the environment spur it on? Could some gathered seeds stored outdoors have accidentally taken root and become the first crop field? Or did the first "crops" spring up after some seeds left in a rubbish heap sprouted?

Naturally, this change didn't occur all at once. First, small groups of people settled down together, forming early villages that eventually grew into towns and cities. As these communities continued over the years, they changed. Societies complete with a written language, a code of law, and advanced technologies developed.

One of the places this first occurred was an area in what is now the Middle East known as Mesopotamia—a land between

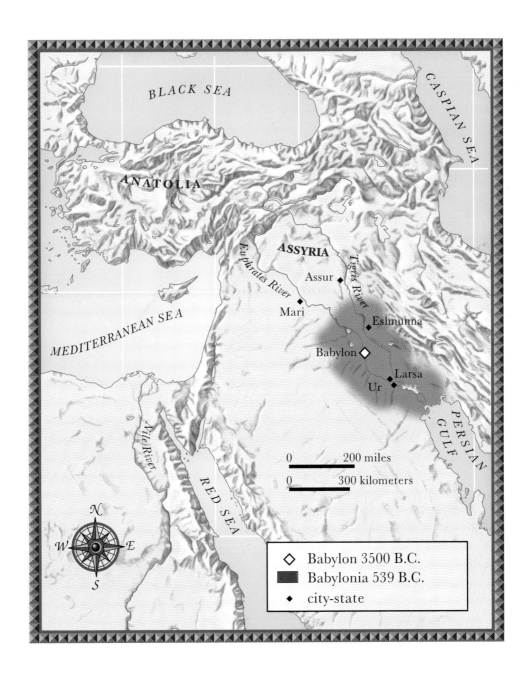

BLACK SEA

CASPIAN SEA

ANATOLIA

ASSYRIA

Assur

Euphrates River

Tigris River

Mari

Eshnunna

MEDITERRANEAN SEA

Babylon

Larsa

Ur

Nile River

PERSIAN GULF

RED SEA

0   200 miles

0   300 kilometers

N
W   E
S

◇ Babylon 3500 B.C.
▨ Babylonia 539 B.C.
♦ city-state

where the Tigris and Euphrates rivers empty into the Persian Gulf.[1] There on a hot, dry, windswept plain, now referred to as a "cradle of civilization," some of the earliest cultures arose. Among these was Assyria, an area on the upper Tigris River in northern Mesopotamia. Another important region known as Sumer occupied 10,000 square miles (26,000 square kilometers) in southern Mesopotamia. Sumer later became Babylonia—a third accomplished Mesopotamian civilization.

The borders between these ancient areas were not always precisely drawn. Wars, political takeovers, and population shifts all served to intermingle the various peoples in the vicinity. Yet these three cultures remain distinct for their important contributions to the world. Ancient Mesopotamians invented the wheel, studied the stars and other heavenly bodies, and achieved important developments in mathematics, medicine, and architecture. They built cities, made advances in art and literature, and were the first people to develop a legal code.

For many years little was known about ancient Mesopotamia. Rain, floods, shifting sands, and other natural occurrences had erased its narrow, winding streets, and its courtyards, religious towers, and magnificent palaces. But by the mid-nineteenth century, archaeologists unearthed the clay tablets, pottery, tools, and building ruins of the Mesopotamians. To accomplish this, archaeological teams dug through huge mounds of soil, stripping away numerous layers of earth. Photographers took pictures of any articles found, while archaeologists interpreted when and how the various items were used. Specialists in ancient languages translated the writings on clay tablets, providing even more information on societies of the past. These clues enabled them to piece together a fascinating picture of the extremely advanced and industrious peoples who once inhabited this "cradle of civilization."

Named for a Babylonian goddess, the Ishtar Gate in the city of Babylon was the setting of many grand processions. In the upper-left corner of the picture can be seen the Hanging Gardens of Babylon.

BABYLONIA

icture a magnificent city in the ancient Near East, a center of life filled with stunning temples, towers, and palaces. Airy courtyards dot the landscape—there's even a lush green garden overflowing with plants and trees in this desert haven. Beauty and color seem to greet your eye at every turn. Bright yellow, red, and white wall tiles are used to create images of dragons and rows of lions on city walls and gates.

Yet this city is more than just dazzling to see. It is also a cultural center where painting, sculpture, literature, and music thrive. Scientists also live here, anxious to advance their studies and research. This city is not an imaginary paradise. It's Babylon, the capital of the ancient land of Babylonia.

While Babylonia was among the earliest advanced civilizations, its capital city of Babylon wasn't always as majestic as it eventually became. In about 3000 B.C., Babylon was just one

Hammurabi was a strong leader whose contributions to Babylonian society made it one of the most splendid and advanced in the ancient world.

of many loosely connected city-states ruled by the Amorites, a group of desert people descended from nomadic Syrian and Arabian tribes. The various city-states existed in an uneasy alliance. Any family or cultural ties between the different Amorite sheikhs, or rulers, did little to rein in their lust for power and possessions. At times, petty jealousies and conflicts between the Amorite city-states erupted into full-scale battles. The victor usually considered his success a step toward gaining control of the entire region.

Hammurabi was sixth in a line of Amorite sheikhs ruling the city-state of Babylon. When he took the throne in 1750 B.C. his work was cut out for him. As the sheikh of Babylon, Hammurabi found himself surrounded by dangerously cunning rival city-states. These included Larsa—a powerful Amorite city-state that already dominated a number of city-states to the south of Babylon. Another of Babylon's powerful rivals was Mari, which lay to the northwest in what today is Syria. But Hammurabi was particularly concerned about two especially warlike city-states to the north known as Eshnunna and Assur.

Being a skilled statesman and militarist, Hammurabi knew he would have to wait and fortify his position before launching a strike. So for the first twenty-five years of his forty-two-year reign, he entered into a number of advantageous alliances with other city-states. These relationships served to both keep enemies at a safe distance as well as enhance his own city-state of Babylon through favorable trade agreements.

However, Hammurabi never hesitated to break these ties when it benefited him to do so. Following his thirtieth year as Babylon's sheikh, he ordered a surprise attack on the city-state of Larsa. Hammurabi emerged as its conqueror as well as head of most of central and southern Mesopotamia. Within three years Hammurabi also destroyed the rival city-state of Mari. This victory allowed him to seize control of western Mesopotamia, which Mari had long dominated.

At that point, Hammurabi needed only to overtake the north to secure all of Mesopotamia. But the brilliant military strategist knew that this might prove extremely difficult. Much of northern Mesopotamia was controlled by Assyria, a country of fierce warriors that placed great emphasis on military might. Yet, during Hammurabi's reign, Assyrian strength had declined somewhat and this once fearsome power had become increasingly dependent on its alliance with the northern Mesopotamian city-state of Eshnunna. After Hammurabi attacked and conquered Eshnunna, the Assyrians had no choice but to accept his rule. Like the rest of Mesopotamia, they were at least temporarily under his control.

Hammurabi had realized his goal of ruling a united Mesopotamia with Babylon as its capital city. Having brought Babylon to a new level of greatness, the whole area came to be known as Babylonia. Proud of his achievement, Hammurabi proclaimed that Babylonia was "supreme in the world." He described his position and that of Babylonia as being "as firm as those of heaven and earth."[2] And during his lifetime, this appeared to be true.

HAMMURABI'S BABYLONIA

While Hammurabi remained on the throne, Babylonia thrived. Babylonian scientists made important strides in astronomy. Mathematicians achieved advances in algebra and geometry and devised tables to quickly calculate the square and cube roots of numbers. Babylonian writers composed epics and poetry, while sculptors created statues and scenes in stone and clay depicting the Babylonian way of life.

Agriculture and trade were strong in the area as well. Hammurabi maintained the region's complex irrigation systems, ensuring that the farmlands stayed fertile. With the ample crops produced, there was more than enough food. The excess was usually stored for later use or traded for the raw materials that the Babylonians needed.

Although the region had long-established trade routes, trade flourished during this period. Located on the banks of the Euphrates River, Babylonia's capital city of Babylon became an important trading center. Babylonian traders regularly traveled west to Syria and other lands as well as south to regions along the Persian Gulf. They traded grain and woven cloth for wood with which to build furniture and ships. The traders also returned from their journeys with gold, silver, precious gems, and livestock.

The profitable trade market helped Babylonia's economy grow and prosper. A wide assortment of craftspeople did quite well there. Metalworkers used imported copper, iron, and tin to construct farm equipment, building parts, and weapons for war. Since there were few trees in the region, Babylonian carpenters relied on the wood brought in by traders to build a broad range of items. Other Babylonian craftspeople included leather workers who made shoes, belts, and water bags, and basket weavers who produced containers, mats, bedding, and even small boats. Babylonian jewelers designed beautiful necklaces, bracelets, earrings, and decorative daggers, while other artisans created magnificent wall murals and a variety of decorative items.

Elaborate ornaments were essential to enhance the spectacular temples and palaces existing in Hammurabi's Babylonia. Kings, high priests, wealthy upper-class families, and some well-placed government officials had splendid homes and wore the finest garments. But, of course, not everyone lived in luxury—the various craftsworkers, tradespeople, clerks, farmers, and merchants lived considerably less lavishly. Their more modest homes stood along the narrow twisting streets of Babylon and other Babylonian cities. These houses usually consisted of several rooms built around an open courtyard.

Slaves were on the lowest rung of Babylonian society. But Babylonian slaves did enjoy some rights. Once their duties for their masters were completed, they were permitted to work elsewhere and keep their wages. Slaves were also allowed to own property and enter into business agreements. If they were able to save enough money, they could even buy their freedom.

Babylonian women also had more rights and freedoms than females in other ancient societies. While their fathers still usually picked their husbands, married Babylonian women remained somewhat independent. They were permitted to have their own property and money.

In many ways Hammurabi strove to make Babylonian society just. Besides uniting Mesopotamia during his reign, Hammurabi is best known for the legal code he devised. The ancient ruler claimed that the gods had instructed him to write these early legal statutes (laws) "to make justice appear in the land," and so that "the strong may not oppress the weak."[3]

Hammurabi's detailed code covered a broad range of situations. The complete legal code consisted of about 280 sections and dealt with such issues as trade disputes, wages for herdsmen and farm laborers, penalties for destroying or stealing property, and rates for renting a boat, wagon, or farm animal for a specific time. There also were portions covering marriage, divorce, adoption, inheritance, and assault. Still other sections delved into penalties for unsatisfactory professional services, and the treatment and sale of slaves.

The following are some examples from Hammurabi's code of justice:

- A builder who sells a poorly constructed house that collapses and kills its owner may be put to death. If the owner's son rather than the owner is killed in the collapse, the builder's son may be put to death.
- A surgeon who operates on a gentleman (a member of the wealthy upper class) and saves the patient's life will be paid ten shekels (coins) of silver for that service. If the patient is a commoner, the surgeon will be given five shekels. If the patient is a slave, the surgeon can expect to receive two shekels of silver. However, if the doctor makes a surgical error resulting in the patient's death, the surgeon's hand may be cut off.
- Someone who steals another person's slave or hides a runaway slave intending to keep that individual as his own slave may be put to death.
- If someone helping to put out a fire loots (steals something from the premises), that individual may be thrown into the fire.

Hammurabi's code of laws was carved on a pillar and placed in a temple for all to see. At the top of the monument, Hammurabi (left) stands before the sun god Shamash.

- A man who lies while serving as a witness in a court case involving the death penalty may also be put to death. If a witness lies while testifying in a property dispute, that individual may have to pay the same costs as the person who loses the case.
- If, due to crop failure resulting from either a flood or drought, someone is unable to pay interest on a debt, he may be excused from the interest payment that year.
- If a son strikes his father, his hand may be cut off.
- If a person destroys a gentleman's eye, his eye may be destroyed in turn. If he breaks a gentleman's bone, the same bone in his body may be broken. However, if a commoner's eye is destroyed or his bone broken, the offender may only be required to pay a fine. If a slave's eye is destroyed or his bone broken, the guilty person must pay half the slave's sale price to his owner.
- If a slave strikes a free man, his ear may be cut off.
- If two equals engage in a fair fight and one is injured, the person causing the injury may have to pay for the other's medical treatment. However, he cannot be punished further for having caused the injury.
- If an ox unexpectedly gouges a man, causing his death, no claim may be made against the animal's owner. However, the owner of an animal that habitually gouges must restrain his animal's movement or remove or cap the ox's horns. If the owner fails to take these precautions and the animal gouges someone, the owner must pay a substantial fine.

- If a wife's poor behavior publicly disgraces her husband, he can be rid of her with no penalty to himself. However, he must first prove his claim in court. Once his claim is recognized, he can either divorce her or marry another woman, reducing the status of his first wife to that of household slave girl.

- If a woman is disgraced by her husband, she can also go to court. If her accusations are adequately proven, she can leave her husband and take her dowry (the property or sum of money a wife brings to her husband in marriage) with her.

- A husband cannot divorce a sickly wife because of her illness. He is required to care for her in their home for the rest of her life. But if the woman wishes to leave on her own accord, she is free to do so and can take her full dowry with her.

- A man can leave property to his wife rather than his son. However, a woman is not allowed to sell property willed to her by her husband. At her death, all she owns goes to her sons.

While Hammurabi's laws covered numerous specific incidents, no legal code could possibly deal with every dispute or problem that might arise. Hammurabi intended that the reasoning behind his prescribed legal penalties would extend to similar situations arising at that time and in the future. The ancient ruler wanted his code to be the law of the land in the broadest sense of the word. He advised all future Babylonian rulers to refer to his regulations in their decision making. He wrote:

To the end of days, forever, may the king who happens to be in the land observe the words of justice which I have inscribed. . . . If that man has the sanction [of the gods] and so is able to give his land justice, let him pay heed to the words which I have written . . . and let that show him the accustomed way, the way to follow, the land's judgments which I have judged and the land's decisions which I have decided.[4]

Some of Hammurabi's laws may seem particularly harsh by present-day standards. Depending on the offense, people might be put to death, lose an eye or limb, have their bones broken, be tortured, or have their children put to death. Yet it's important to view these laws within the framework of the time and place in which they were written. Hammurabi unified legal practices throughout Babylonia. This was an important step toward creating a society in which everyone's rights were recognized to some degree, regardless of class.

KASSITE RULE

Although Hammurabi predicted that Babylonia would exist forever, history tells another story. Soon after his death in 1708 B.C., the ruler's empire began to crumble. Hammurabi's son did his best to hold things together, but before long revolts broke out in many of the areas his father had conquered. Unable to quell these ongoing rebellions, Babylonia lost its southern and northern provinces. Eventually Hammurabi's former domain shrank from nearly all of Mesopotamia to little more than the capital city of Babylon along with some surrounding territory. Hammurabi's descendants occupied the throne for more than a hundred years. But rather than expand Babylonia's borders as their famous ancestor had, they focused on internal matters.

In about 1600 B.C., Babylonia was invaded by the Hittites, a people from Anatolia (Asia Minor) who returned to their homeland after sacking Babylonia. Weakened and demoralized by the attack, Babylonia was ripe for conquest. The Kassites, a group from the Zagros Mountains to the east of Babylonia, seized the opportunity and invaded.

The Kassites ruled Babylonia for nearly four hundred years, from about 1595 to 1157 B.C.—considerably longer than any other dynasty (line of kings). But the Kassites' rule was hardly oppressive. These invaders adopted Babylonia's culture and became fully absorbed into the Babylonian way of life. As they were careful not to tread on the already established rights of Babylonian citizens, they never had to deal with rebellions. And, maintaining internal stability over the years, the Kassites successfully reunited all of Babylonia. They were also able to retake the territory to the south, which had been lost following Hammurabi's death.

While ruling Babylonia, the Kassites were especially active in encouraging international trade. They established an ongoing trade agreement with Egypt that provided for a number of caravans carrying trade goods to travel between the two countries. During the thirteenth and fourteenth centuries B.C., trade also blossomed between Babylonia and Assyria—the now strong empire-building nation that once had been controlled by Babylonia. Babylonia even imported precious gems from such distant places as India and Afghanistan by way of Iran.

From the beginning of the fourteenth century B.C. on, there was also a great deal of rebuilding in Babylonia. Internal peace allowed funds and energy to be put into restoring the area. New prosperous towns sprang up, and the temples and other structures at important ancient cities were restored as well. Some of the outer walls of the temples were decorated with attractive paintings and sculpture.

It was also a time of religious renewal in Babylonia. From about 1200 B.C. there had been a trend toward worshiping one god rather than many. Now, the Babylonians viewed the god Marduk as the ultimate supreme being and made him their national god. A Babylonian myth about how the world was created details Marduk's rise as the chief god. Known as the Epic of Creation, the story was written on seven clay tablets and publicly recited in Babylon annually on the fourth day of the New Year festival. It described the ceremony at which Marduk was appointed to his high position in this way:

The great gods all of them who determines destinies . . . filled the Hall of Assembly. . . . They embraced each other . . . they held conversation . . . they ate bread, they drank wine . . . they were carefree. . . . For Marduk, their avenger . . . they set him on a princely throne [and proclaimed] "You are the most honored one among the great gods, your decree is law. From this very day your command shall be unalterable. . . . No one among the gods shall overstep your bounds. . . . We have given you kingship over the whole universe; sit in the Assembly and let your word be supreme!" They rejoiced and gave blessings, "Marduk is King." [5]

In addition to the emphasis on religion, there was also a burst of literary activity during the Kassites' Babylonian reign. Myths, epics, and hymns to both the gods and rulers were composed. Other new works included compositions exploring such issues as proper conduct and sound beliefs. These pieces were often referred to as Wisdom Literature. Older works were not forgotten, as scribes of the time spent seemingly endless hours carefully copying ancient texts.

Special schools existed to teach the scribal art. A young person attending one of these institutions needed both patience and dedication. Besides learning to copy clearly and precisely, students were also required to memorize long lists of names, terms, and phrases. School hours were extremely long, and schoolmasters accepted nothing short of excellence from their students. A young person wishing to become a scribe could expect to attend a scribal academy for many years. According to one ancient text describing the necessary training, "You sat in the Tablet House [scribal school] from the days of your youth to maturity."[6]

Babylonian scribes tended to be held in high esteem as they were needed for more than copying literary texts. Qualified scribes were found in a number of professions, although

Marduk, the god of creation, was the most powerful of the Babylonian gods.

Using a writing style known as cuneiform, Babylonian scribes recorded events, laws, and business transactions on both stone and animal skins. These scribes (left) are tallying the booty and the slain from a military conquest. These tablets (opposite below) are inscribed with a mathematics test.

most young Babylonian scribes entered the specific field of their fathers. Many scribes could be found in the marketplace, recording the continuous business transactions occurring there. Others worked for the temple or palace, keeping the temple accounts in order or writing out royal proclamations. Still other scribes accompanied troops on military campaigns. Field generals needed scribes to write the dispatches sent home. Scribes were used also to keep an account of the rations and supplies needed by soldiers on the march.

Some Babylonian scribes became extremely well known and respected for their ability. In the years to come many scribal families would trace their lineage (family line) back to a scribe who began to actively practice his art during this period of Kassite rule.

A FLEETING SPLENDOR

Although Babylonia enjoyed a period of peace and renewal under the Kassite dynasty, this peaceful period didn't last. In about 1157 B.C. the Elamites, from the south in Iran, invaded the area. After overthrowing the last Kassite king, they ruthlessly plundered Babylonia's major cities. To humiliate the defeated Babylonians even further, the Elamites carried off some of their most valued national treasures. This included the 7-foot 6-inch (228-centimeter) monument bearing Hammurabi's legal code as well as a statue of the national god, Marduk.

Yet despite their defeat, the Babylonians managed to pull together their resources. A new Babylonian dynasty arose that demonstrated some of the country's former might. One ruler, Nebuchadrezzar I, drove out the remaining Elamite soldiers. Then he attacked Elam itself and recaptured the monument

Although the Babylonians were known more for cultural pursuits rather than conquests, they maintained a strong army. This warrior and his horse are dressed in typical Babylonian fashion.

with Hammurabi's code, along with the statue of Marduk taken during the Elamites' plunder of Babylonia. This surge of Babylonian strength continued with another Babylonian leader, who invaded Assyria to the north. The Babylonians actually came within 20 miles (32 kilometers) of Assyria's capital city, Assur, before being turned back.

But before long the balance of power in the region shifted. By the beginning of the eleventh century B.C., Babylonia had begun a spiraling decline that continued for the next four hundred years. Meanwhile, Assyria's power soared. Unlike the Babylonians, who had long been interested in culture, the Assyrians were largely focused on military might and conquest. Babylonia was not left untouched by the ambitions of its empire-building neighbor to the north. In the eighth century the Assyrian ruler Tiglath-Pileser III overthrew the Babylonian king, imposing his rule on the region.

But Assyria's conquests did not last. The territory conquered by this aggressive power proved too widespread to control. Continuously trying to quell revolts on several fronts, Assyria's fighting force was weakened and the country's resources were depleted.

Toward the end of the seventh century B.C. the Babylonian forces joined with the Medes, a people from the Iranian plateau, to defeat Assyria. Now once again an independent nation, Babylonia began to grow and prosper. In what is known as the New Babylonian Empire, Babylonia regained control

This rendition of the Tower of Babel is from a sixteenth-century book. It is believed that the Babylonian ziggurat Etemenankia was the Tower of Babel referred to in the Bible.

over Mesopotamia as well as much of the conquered territory lost by Assyria.

A great deal of credit for Babylonia's success during this time goes to the monarch Nebuchadrezzar II, who reigned from 605 B.C. to 562 B.C. Nebuchadrezzar II was an outstanding military leader who did not hesitate to take on new challenges. When the Egyptians advanced into the Middle East, Nebuchadrezzar II defeated their forces on the upper Euphrates River. He also controlled all of Syria and part of Palestine (now Israel). But Nebuchadrezzar II may be best known for his siege of Jerusalem in 597 B.C., followed by his deportation of the Hebrew people to Babylonia. The Hebrews were forced to leave their homeland to prevent them from rebelling against Nebuchadrezzar II's control of their territory. The deportation was carried out in three phases, and is often referred to as the Babylonian Exile. The Hebrews were not able to return to their land for about seventy years.

Nebuchadrezzar II could be ruthless in battle, but he was much more than just a militarist. He was also responsible for bringing back the splendor and glory in Babylonia, which had not existed since Hammurabi's time. Nebuchadrezzar II turned Babylonia's capital city of Babylon into a magnificent cultural center. As in other Babylonian cities, he restored Babylon's temples. This meant splendidly rebuilding the seven-story-high ziggurat (temple tower) known as Etemenankia, or "House of the Platform Between Heaven and Earth." Some suspect that

this tower was actually the Tower of Babel referred to in the Bible. The companion temple complex to this magnificent tower was called Esagila. Nebuchadrezzar II displayed his devotion to the god Marduk by restoring the temple with fine woods, precious metals, and valuable gems. Marduk's main chapel within Esagila dazzled the eye. It was a chamber measuring about 66 by 132 feet (20 by 40 meters), which King Nebuchadrezzar II ordered overlaid entirely with gold. Inside were golden images of Marduk and his attendants decorated with magnificent shining gems.

Nebuchadrezzar II had several palaces. Besides serving as a royal residence, the main palace also housed the troops and served as an administrative center from which affairs of state were conducted. Nebuchadrezzar II restored all the palaces in Babylon. He used newly baked bricks to replace the less attractive sun-dried bricks of the past. He used imported polished cedar beams for the roofs and adorned the walls with colorful glazed tiles. Nebuchadrezzar II further decorated the buildings with ornaments and detailing in solid gold and silver, using various precious stones as accents.

Covered with words in cuneiform, this sculpture shows Assyrian king Assurbanipal rebuilding Esagila, the companion temple to Etemenankia, after an Assyrian bombardment of Babylon.

Perhaps Nebuchadrezzar II's best-known project to beautify Babylon was the Hanging Gardens of Babylon. This was a magnificent piece of landscaping consisting of a series of earth-covered terraces that rose to a height of about 75 feet (23 meters). A vast array of trees and shrubs were planted on the terraces. The Hanging Gardens were kept lush and green with special irrigation systems designed to provide an ongoing water supply. The result was a stunning green spectacle in a desert land. The sight was so overwhelming that the Hanging Gardens are considered one of the great wonders of the ancient world.[7]

Since he was a fighter as well as a ruler, Nebuchadrezzar II knew the importance of keeping his magnificent city secure. As enemies in these times frequently attacked by scaling a major city's walls, Nebuchadrezzar II was determined to make that exceedingly hard to do. He began by constructing a double wall of unbaked bricks to encircle Babylon. Both portions of the wall were very sturdy, with the inner section more than 21 feet (6 meters) thick. Atop both the inner and outer walls were towers large enough for a person to stand in. These were battle stations from which an archer might shoot an arrow if the city was under attack.

To make it still harder to invade Babylon, Nebuchadrezzar II had a moat built around the outer wall. While this might seem like an unusual fortification in a desert location, water for the moat was pumped in from the Euphrates River. The bridges used to cross the moat in peacetime could be quickly dismantled

Created by Nebuchadrezzar II, the Hanging Gardens of Babylon were a landscaping marvel and one of the wonders of the ancient world.

if the city were under siege. Since Babylon could be entered through any of eight gates, Nebuchadrezzar II fortified these entranceways by installing a massive bronze door at each. As a further safeguard, he built a third great wall along the eastern portion of Babylon. Nebuchadrezzar II strengthened this line of defense with another moat.

But despite his best efforts, the power and grandeur that Babylon and Babylonia experienced under Nebuchadrezzar II was short-lived. The New Babylonian Empire lasted only about seventy-five years. For the most part, the rulers following Nebuchadrezzar II lacked his military and political prowess and decisiveness. As several seemed quick to change their positions on important matters, these monarchs were sometimes viewed as weak and wavering. And history ultimately proved them unable to maintain the glorious empire they inherited.

THE FINAL FALL

The decline that Babylonia experienced following Nebuchadrezzar II's death continued. The last Babylonian king, Nabonidus, lost public support when he attempted to substitute another god for Marduk. The religious unrest and dissension he created helped pave the way for the next conqueror—Cyrus, the king of Persia. Cyrus was an outstanding statesman known for respecting the rights and ways of those he conquered. When he entered Babylonia in 539 B.C. he met little resistance. That was how Babylonia ended. The once great power and civilization became an unrecognizable part of the Persian empire. Babylonia never emerged as a separate and distinct country again.

In the centuries that followed, the area was invaded by a number of foreign powers, including the Greeks, Arabs, and

Turks. When the Turks were defeated by the British in World War I, Britain took control of the region. After renaming the area Iraq, they established an Arab-led government under firm British control. However, Iraq won its independence from Britain in 1932.

For a time, Alexander the Great made Babylon the capital of his vast empire. This woodcut shows him entering the city.

Today the land that was formerly Babylonia lies in southeastern Iraq. Though their country is no longer on the map, the advances achieved by the ancient Babylonians in art, law, and science had a vast impact on future societies for centuries to come.

IMPORTANT DATES

1792–1750 B.C.	Hammurabi rules Babylon and eventually brings most of Mesopotamia under his control.
1600 B.C.	Babylonia is invaded by the Hittites, who ransack and plunder the area before leaving it.
1595 B.C.	The Kassites, a group from the Zagros Mountains to the east, invade Babylonia and rule for nearly four hundred years.
1157 B.C.	The Elamites invade Babylonia and overthrow the last Kassite ruler.
1124 B.C.	Nebuchadrezzar I drives the Elamites out of Babylonia.
1100 B.C.	Babylonian soldiers invade Assyria but are turned back just 20 miles (32 kilometers) from Assyria's capital city of Assur.

745 B.C.	Assyrian ruler Tiglath-Pileser III overthrows the Babylonian king, imposing his rule on the region.
605–562 B.C.	Nebuchadrezzar II restores Babylonia to greatness, extending its territory and refurbishing its palaces and temples.
539 B.C.	Cyrus, king of Persia, conquers Babylonia, making it part of the Persian empire.

NOTES

1. Arthur Cotterell, ed., *The Encyclopedia of Civilization* (New York: Mayflower Books, Inc., 1980), p. 72.

2. Samuel Noah Kramer and the Editors of Time-Life Books, *Cradle of Civilization* (Alexandria, VA: Time-Life Books, 1978), p. 53.

3. Kramer, p. 53.

4. H.W.F. Saggs, *Everyday Life in Babylonia & Assyria* (New York: G. P. Putnam's Sons, 1967), p. 146.

5. H.W.F. Saggs, *The Greatness That Was Babylon* (New York: Hawthorn Books, 1962), p. 414.

6. H.W.F. Saggs, *Babylonians* (Norman: University of Oklahoma Press, 1995), p. 149.

7. Joan Oates, *Babylon* (London: Thames and Hudson Ltd., 1979), p. 151.

GLOSSARY

algebra–a form of math in which symbols are used to represent any set of numbers in calculations

alliance–a formal treaty or agreement between states or countries

artisan–a trained or skilled worker or craftsperson

astronomy–the study of the stars, moon, planets, and other bodies in space

city-state–a city that functions as though it were an independent state or country

deity–a god

dowry–the property or sum of money a wife brings to her husband in marriage

dynasty–a line of kings or rulers

epic–a long formal verse celebrating a heroic event or achievement

geometry–a form of math that deals with the measurements and relationships between points, lines, angles, and surfaces

gouge–to scoop or tear out

haven–a safe, protected place

irrigation–a means through which water is channeled to arid (dry) land

lineage–family line

militarist–someone concerned with the army and battles

moat–a wide, deep, water-filled ditch surrounding a castle or city wall

myth–an imaginary person, place, or story

nomadic–wandering

offspring–children

province–an outlying region some distance from the capital or major cities

ration–a fixed portion of food or provisions that is allotted daily to a soldier

rival–a person, group, or country that strives to outdo a competitor

scribe–a person who in ancient times copied manuscripts or texts, or kept records

sheikh–the ruler or chief of an Arab tribe

Wisdom Literature–a type of ancient composition in which issues such as proper conduct and beliefs were explored

ziggurat–an ancient pyramid-shaped temple tower

FURTHER READING

Avi-Yonah, Michael. *Dig This! How Archaeologists Uncover Our Past.* Minneapolis: Runestone Press, 1993.

Corbishley, Mike. *Secret Cities.* New York: Lodestar, 1989.

Foster, Leila M. *The Sumerians.* Danbury, CT: Franklin Watts, 1990.

Gallant, Roy A. *Lost Cities.* Danbury, CT: Franklin Watts, 1985.

Goldenstein, Joyce. *Lost Cities.* Cliffside, NJ: Enslow Publishers, 1996.

Moss, Carol. *Science in Ancient Mesopotamia.* Danbury, CT: Franklin Watts, 1988.

Oliphant, Margaret. *The Earliest Civilizations.* New York: Facts on File, 1993.

Russell, Paul. *Writing & Arithmetic: Ancient Civilizations.* New York: Tamborine Books, 1994.

Trease, Geoffrey. *Hidden Treasure.* New York: Lodestar Books, 1989.

INDEX